COPYRIGHT © 2022 BY TAM PREJUSA. ISBN#979-8-88627-032-7
PRINTED IN THE USA
ALL RIGHTS RESERVED. UNLESS OTHERWISE NOTED,
NO PART OF THIS BOOK MAY BE REPRODUCED, STORED IN A RETRIEVAL SYSTEM,
OR TRANSMITTED IN ANY FORM OR BY ANY MEANS, INCLUDING ELECTRONIC,
MECHANICAL, PHOTOCOPYING, RECORDING OR OTHERWISE, WITHOUT
EXPRESS WRITTEN PERMISSION FROM THE PUBLISHER.

Create something everyday

This Journal Book Belongs To:

Thank you for following along with me on my adventures! - Tam

DATE: _____

WHAT I LEARNED TODAY...

WHAT I WANT TO LEARN TO DO AND TO BE BETTER AT...

MY CREATIVE IDEAS AND PROJECTS...

PLAN AND ACTION (What I need to do to make it happen)...

DATE: _____

I AM GRATEFUL FOR...

MY THOUGHTS AND FEELINGS...

MY DREAM AND WISH...

DATE: _____

WHAT I LEARNED TODAY...

WHAT I WANT TO LEARN TO DO AND TO BE BETTER AT...

MY CREATIVE IDEAS AND PROJECTS...

PLAN AND ACTION (What I need to do to make it happen)...

DATE: _____

I AM GRATEFUL FOR...

MY THOUGHTS AND FEELINGS...

MY DREAM AND WISH...

DATE: _____

WHAT I LEARNED TODAY...

WHAT I WANT TO LEARN TO DO AND TO BE BETTER AT...

MY CREATIVE IDEAS AND PROJECTS...

PLAN AND ACTION (What I need to do to make it happen)...

DATE: _____

I AM GRATEFUL FOR...

MY THOUGHTS AND FEELINGS...

MY DREAM AND WISH...

DATE: _____

WHAT I LEARNED TODAY...

WHAT I WANT TO LEARN TO DO AND TO BE BETTER AT...

MY CREATIVE IDEAS AND PROJECTS...

PLAN AND ACTION (What I need to do to make it happen)...

DATE: _____

I AM GRATEFUL FOR...

MY THOUGHTS AND FEELINGS...

MY DREAM AND WISH...

DATE: _____

WHAT I LEARNED TODAY...

WHAT I WANT TO LEARN TO DO AND TO BE BETTER AT...

MY CREATIVE IDEAS AND PROJECTS...

PLAN AND ACTION (What I need to do to make it happen)...

DATE: _____

I AM GRATEFUL FOR...

MY THOUGHTS AND FEELINGS...

MY DREAM AND WISH...

DATE: _____

WHAT I LEARNED TODAY...

WHAT I WANT TO LEARN TO DO AND TO BE BETTER AT...

MY CREATIVE IDEAS AND PROJECTS...

PLAN AND ACTION (What I need to do to make it happen)...

DATE: _____

I AM GRATEFUL FOR...

MY THOUGHTS AND FEELINGS...

MY DREAM AND WISH...

DATE: _____

WHAT I LEARNED TODAY...

WHAT I WANT TO LEARN TO DO AND TO BE BETTER AT...

MY CREATIVE IDEAS AND PROJECTS...

PLAN AND ACTION (What I need to do to make it happen)...

DATE: _____

I AM GRATEFUL FOR...

MY THOUGHTS AND FEELINGS...

MY DREAM AND WISH...

DATE: _____

WHAT I LEARNED TODAY...

WHAT I WANT TO LEARN TO DO AND TO BE BETTER AT...

MY CREATIVE IDEAS AND PROJECTS...

PLAN AND ACTION (What I need to do to make it happen)...

DATE: _____

I AM GRATEFUL FOR...

MY THOUGHTS AND FEELINGS...

MY DREAM AND WISH...

DATE: _____

WHAT I LEARNED TODAY...

WHAT I WANT TO LEARN TO DO AND TO BE BETTER AT...

MY CREATIVE IDEAS AND PROJECTS...

PLAN AND ACTION (What I need to do to make it happen)...

DATE: _____

I AM GRATEFUL FOR...

MY THOUGHTS AND FEELINGS...

MY DREAM AND WISH...

DATE: _____

WHAT I LEARNED TODAY...

WHAT I WANT TO LEARN TO DO AND TO BE BETTER AT...

MY CREATIVE IDEAS AND PROJECTS...

PLAN AND ACTION (What I need to do to make it happen)...

DATE: _____

I AM GRATEFUL FOR...

MY THOUGHTS AND FEELINGS...

MY DREAM AND WISH...

DATE: _____

WHAT I LEARNED TODAY...

WHAT I WANT TO LEARN TO DO AND TO BE BETTER AT...

MY CREATIVE IDEAS AND PROJECTS...

PLAN AND ACTION (What I need to do to make it happen)...

DATE: _____

I AM GRATEFUL FOR...

MY THOUGHTS AND FEELINGS...

MY DREAM AND WISH...

DATE: _____

WHAT I LEARNED TODAY...

WHAT I WANT TO LEARN TO DO AND TO BE BETTER AT...

MY CREATIVE IDEAS AND PROJECTS...

PLAN AND ACTION (What I need to do to make it happen)...

DATE: _____

I AM GRATEFUL FOR...

MY THOUGHTS AND FEELINGS...

MY DREAM AND WISH...

DATE: _____

WHAT I LEARNED TODAY...

WHAT I WANT TO LEARN TO DO AND TO BE BETTER AT...

MY CREATIVE IDEAS AND PROJECTS...

PLAN AND ACTION (What I need to do to make it happen)...

DATE: _____

I AM GRATEFUL FOR...

MY THOUGHTS AND FEELINGS...

MY DREAM AND WISH...

DATE: _____

WHAT I LEARNED TODAY...

WHAT I WANT TO LEARN TO DO AND TO BE BETTER AT...

MY CREATIVE IDEAS AND PROJECTS...

PLAN AND ACTION (What I need to do to make it happen)...

DATE: _____

I AM GRATEFUL FOR...

MY THOUGHTS AND FEELINGS...

MY DREAM AND WISH...

DATE: _____

WHAT I LEARNED TODAY...

WHAT I WANT TO LEARN TO DO AND TO BE BETTER AT...

MY CREATIVE IDEAS AND PROJECTS...

PLAN AND ACTION (What I need to do to make it happen)...

DATE: _____

I AM GRATEFUL FOR...

MY THOUGHTS AND FEELINGS...

MY DREAM AND WISH...

DATE: _____

WHAT I LEARNED TODAY...

WHAT I WANT TO LEARN TO DO AND TO BE BETTER AT...

MY CREATIVE IDEAS AND PROJECTS...

PLAN AND ACTION (What I need to do to make it happen)...

DATE: _____

I AM GRATEFUL FOR...

MY THOUGHTS AND FEELINGS...

MY DREAM AND WISH...

DATE: _____

WHAT I LEARNED TODAY...

WHAT I WANT TO LEARN TO DO AND TO BE BETTER AT...

MY CREATIVE IDEAS AND PROJECTS...

PLAN AND ACTION (What I need to do to make it happen)...

DATE: _____

I AM GRATEFUL FOR...

MY THOUGHTS AND FEELINGS...

MY DREAM AND WISH...

DATE: _____

WHAT I LEARNED TODAY...

WHAT I WANT TO LEARN TO DO AND TO BE BETTER AT...

MY CREATIVE IDEAS AND PROJECTS...

PLAN AND ACTION (What I need to do to make it happen)...

DATE: _____

I AM GRATEFUL FOR...

MY THOUGHTS AND FEELINGS...

MY DREAM AND WISH...

DATE: _____

WHAT I LEARNED TODAY...

WHAT I WANT TO LEARN TO DO AND TO BE BETTER AT...

MY CREATIVE IDEAS AND PROJECTS...

PLAN AND ACTION (What I need to do to make it happen)...

DATE: _____

I AM GRATEFUL FOR...

MY THOUGHTS AND FEELINGS...

MY DREAM AND WISH...

DATE: _____

WHAT I LEARNED TODAY...

WHAT I WANT TO LEARN TO DO AND TO BE BETTER AT...

MY CREATIVE IDEAS AND PROJECTS...

PLAN AND ACTION (What I need to do to make it happen)...

DATE: _____

I AM GRATEFUL FOR...

MY THOUGHTS AND FEELINGS...

MY DREAM AND WISH...

DATE: _____

WHAT I LEARNED TODAY...

WHAT I WANT TO LEARN TO DO AND TO BE BETTER AT...

MY CREATIVE IDEAS AND PROJECTS...

PLAN AND ACTION (What I need to do to make it happen)...

DATE: _____

I AM GRATEFUL FOR...

MY THOUGHTS AND FEELINGS...

MY DREAM AND WISH...

DATE: _____

WHAT I LEARNED TODAY...

WHAT I WANT TO LEARN TO DO AND TO BE BETTER AT...

MY CREATIVE IDEAS AND PROJECTS...

PLAN AND ACTION (What I need to do to make it happen)...

DATE: _____

I AM GRATEFUL FOR...

MY THOUGHTS AND FEELINGS...

MY DREAM AND WISH...

DATE: _____

WHAT I LEARNED TODAY...

WHAT I WANT TO LEARN TO DO AND TO BE BETTER AT...

MY CREATIVE IDEAS AND PROJECTS...

PLAN AND ACTION (What I need to do to make it happen)...

DATE: _____

I AM GRATEFUL FOR...

MY THOUGHTS AND FEELINGS...

MY DREAM AND WISH...

DATE: _____

WHAT I LEARNED TODAY...

WHAT I WANT TO LEARN TO DO AND TO BE BETTER AT...

MY CREATIVE IDEAS AND PROJECTS...

PLAN AND ACTION (What I need to do to make it happen)...

DATE: _____

I AM GRATEFUL FOR...

MY THOUGHTS AND FEELINGS...

MY DREAM AND WISH...

DATE: _____

WHAT I LEARNED TODAY...

WHAT I WANT TO LEARN TO DO AND TO BE BETTER AT...

MY CREATIVE IDEAS AND PROJECTS...

PLAN AND ACTION (What I need to do to make it happen)...

DATE: _____

I AM GRATEFUL FOR…

MY THOUGHTS AND FEELINGS…

MY DREAM AND WISH…

DATE: _____

WHAT I LEARNED TODAY...

WHAT I WANT TO LEARN TO DO AND TO BE BETTER AT...

MY CREATIVE IDEAS AND PROJECTS...

PLAN AND ACTION (What I need to do to make it happen)...

DATE: _____

I AM GRATEFUL FOR...

MY THOUGHTS AND FEELINGS...

MY DREAM AND WISH...

DATE: _____

WHAT I LEARNED TODAY...

WHAT I WANT TO LEARN TO DO AND TO BE BETTER AT...

MY CREATIVE IDEAS AND PROJECTS...

PLAN AND ACTION (What I need to do to make it happen)...

DATE: _____

I AM GRATEFUL FOR...

MY THOUGHTS AND FEELINGS...

MY DREAM AND WISH...

DATE: _____

WHAT I LEARNED TODAY...

WHAT I WANT TO LEARN TO DO AND TO BE BETTER AT...

MY CREATIVE IDEAS AND PROJECTS...

PLAN AND ACTION (What I need to do to make it happen)...

DATE: _____

I AM GRATEFUL FOR...

MY THOUGHTS AND FEELINGS...

MY DREAM AND WISH...

DATE: _____

WHAT I LEARNED TODAY...

WHAT I WANT TO LEARN TO DO AND TO BE BETTER AT...

MY CREATIVE IDEAS AND PROJECTS...

PLAN AND ACTION (What I need to do to make it happen)...

DATE: _____

I AM GRATEFUL FOR...

MY THOUGHTS AND FEELINGS...

MY DREAM AND WISH...

DATE: _____

WHAT I LEARNED TODAY...

WHAT I WANT TO LEARN TO DO AND TO BE BETTER AT...

MY CREATIVE IDEAS AND PROJECTS...

PLAN AND ACTION (What I need to do to make it happen)...

DATE: _____

I AM GRATEFUL FOR...

MY THOUGHTS AND FEELINGS...

MY DREAM AND WISH...

DATE: _____

WHAT I LEARNED TODAY...

WHAT I WANT TO LEARN TO DO AND TO BE BETTER AT...

MY CREATIVE IDEAS AND PROJECTS...

PLAN AND ACTION (What I need to do to make it happen)...

DATE: _____

I AM GRATEFUL FOR...

MY THOUGHTS AND FEELINGS...

MY DREAM AND WISH...

DATE: _____

WHAT I LEARNED TODAY...

WHAT I WANT TO LEARN TO DO AND TO BE BETTER AT...

MY CREATIVE IDEAS AND PROJECTS...

PLAN AND ACTION (What I need to do to make it happen)...

DATE: _____

I AM GRATEFUL FOR...

MY THOUGHTS AND FEELINGS...

MY DREAM AND WISH...

DATE: _____

WHAT I LEARNED TODAY...

WHAT I WANT TO LEARN TO DO AND TO BE BETTER AT...

MY CREATIVE IDEAS AND PROJECTS...

PLAN AND ACTION (What I need to do to make it happen)...

DATE: _____

I AM GRATEFUL FOR...

MY THOUGHTS AND FEELINGS...

MY DREAM AND WISH...

DATE: _____

WHAT I LEARNED TODAY...

WHAT I WANT TO LEARN TO DO AND TO BE BETTER AT...

MY CREATIVE IDEAS AND PROJECTS...

PLAN AND ACTION (What I need to do to make it happen)...

DATE: _____

I AM GRATEFUL FOR...

MY THOUGHTS AND FEELINGS...

MY DREAM AND WISH...

DATE: _____

WHAT I LEARNED TODAY...

WHAT I WANT TO LEARN TO DO AND TO BE BETTER AT...

MY CREATIVE IDEAS AND PROJECTS...

PLAN AND ACTION (What I need to do to make it happen)...

DATE: _____

I AM GRATEFUL FOR...

MY THOUGHTS AND FEELINGS...

MY DREAM AND WISH...

DATE: _____

WHAT I LEARNED TODAY...

WHAT I WANT TO LEARN TO DO AND TO BE BETTER AT...

MY CREATIVE IDEAS AND PROJECTS...

PLAN AND ACTION (What I need to do to make it happen)...

DATE: _____

I AM GRATEFUL FOR...

MY THOUGHTS AND FEELINGS...

MY DREAM AND WISH...

DATE: _____

WHAT I LEARNED TODAY...

WHAT I WANT TO LEARN TO DO AND TO BE BETTER AT...

MY CREATIVE IDEAS AND PROJECTS...

PLAN AND ACTION (What I need to do to make it happen)...

DATE: _____

I AM GRATEFUL FOR...

MY THOUGHTS AND FEELINGS...

MY DREAM AND WISH...

DATE: _____

WHAT I LEARNED TODAY...

WHAT I WANT TO LEARN TO DO AND TO BE BETTER AT...

MY CREATIVE IDEAS AND PROJECTS...

PLAN AND ACTION (What I need to do to make it happen)...

DATE: _____

I AM GRATEFUL FOR...

MY THOUGHTS AND FEELINGS...

MY DREAM AND WISH...

DATE: _____

WHAT I LEARNED TODAY...

WHAT I WANT TO LEARN TO DO AND TO BE BETTER AT...

MY CREATIVE IDEAS AND PROJECTS...

PLAN AND ACTION (What I need to do to make it happen)...

DATE: _____

I AM GRATEFUL FOR...

MY THOUGHTS AND FEELINGS...

MY DREAM AND WISH...

DATE: _____

WHAT I LEARNED TODAY...

WHAT I WANT TO LEARN TO DO AND TO BE BETTER AT...

MY CREATIVE IDEAS AND PROJECTS...

PLAN AND ACTION (What I need to do to make it happen)...

DATE: _____

I AM GRATEFUL FOR...

MY THOUGHTS AND FEELINGS...

MY DREAM AND WISH...

DATE: _____

WHAT I LEARNED TODAY...

WHAT I WANT TO LEARN TO DO AND TO BE BETTER AT...

MY CREATIVE IDEAS AND PROJECTS...

PLAN AND ACTION (What I need to do to make it happen)...

DATE: _____

I AM GRATEFUL FOR...

MY THOUGHTS AND FEELINGS...

MY DREAM AND WISH...

DATE: _____

WHAT I LEARNED TODAY...

WHAT I WANT TO LEARN TO DO AND TO BE BETTER AT...

MY CREATIVE IDEAS AND PROJECTS...

PLAN AND ACTION (What I need to do to make it happen)...

DATE: _____

I AM GRATEFUL FOR...

MY THOUGHTS AND FEELINGS...

MY DREAM AND WISH...

DATE: _____

WHAT I LEARNED TODAY...

WHAT I WANT TO LEARN TO DO AND TO BE BETTER AT...

MY CREATIVE IDEAS AND PROJECTS...

PLAN AND ACTION (What I need to do to make it happen)...

DATE: _____

I AM GRATEFUL FOR...

MY THOUGHTS AND FEELINGS...

MY DREAM AND WISH...

DATE: _____

WHAT I LEARNED TODAY...

WHAT I WANT TO LEARN TO DO AND TO BE BETTER AT...

MY CREATIVE IDEAS AND PROJECTS...

PLAN AND ACTION (What I need to do to make it happen)...

DATE: _____

I AM GRATEFUL FOR...

MY THOUGHTS AND FEELINGS...

MY DREAM AND WISH...

DATE: _____

WHAT I LEARNED TODAY...

WHAT I WANT TO LEARN TO DO AND TO BE BETTER AT...

MY CREATIVE IDEAS AND PROJECTS...

PLAN AND ACTION (What I need to do to make it happen)...

DATE: _____

I AM GRATEFUL FOR...

MY THOUGHTS AND FEELINGS...

MY DREAM AND WISH...

DATE: _____

WHAT I LEARNED TODAY...

WHAT I WANT TO LEARN TO DO AND TO BE BETTER AT...

MY CREATIVE IDEAS AND PROJECTS...

PLAN AND ACTION (What I need to do to make it happen)...

DATE: _____

I AM GRATEFUL FOR...

MY THOUGHTS AND FEELINGS...

MY DREAM AND WISH...

DATE: _____

WHAT I LEARNED TODAY...

WHAT I WANT TO LEARN TO DO AND TO BE BETTER AT...

MY CREATIVE IDEAS AND PROJECTS...

PLAN AND ACTION (What I need to do to make it happen)...

DATE: _____

I AM GRATEFUL FOR...

MY THOUGHTS AND FEELINGS...

MY DREAM AND WISH...

DATE: _____

WHAT I LEARNED TODAY...

WHAT I WANT TO LEARN TO DO AND TO BE BETTER AT...

MY CREATIVE IDEAS AND PROJECTS...

PLAN AND ACTION (What I need to do to make it happen)...

DATE: _____

I AM GRATEFUL FOR...

MY THOUGHTS AND FEELINGS...

MY DREAM AND WISH...

DATE: _____

WHAT I LEARNED TODAY...

WHAT I WANT TO LEARN TO DO AND TO BE BETTER AT...

MY CREATIVE IDEAS AND PROJECTS...

PLAN AND ACTION (What I need to do to make it happen)...

DATE: _____

I AM GRATEFUL FOR...

MY THOUGHTS AND FEELINGS...

MY DREAM AND WISH...

DATE: _____

WHAT I LEARNED TODAY...

WHAT I WANT TO LEARN TO DO AND TO BE BETTER AT...

MY CREATIVE IDEAS AND PROJECTS...

PLAN AND ACTION (What I need to do to make it happen)...

DATE: _____

I AM GRATEFUL FOR...

MY THOUGHTS AND FEELINGS...

MY DREAM AND WISH...

DATE: _____

WHAT I LEARNED TODAY...

WHAT I WANT TO LEARN TO DO AND TO BE BETTER AT...

MY CREATIVE IDEAS AND PROJECTS...

PLAN AND ACTION (What I need to do to make it happen)...

DATE: _____

I AM GRATEFUL FOR...

MY THOUGHTS AND FEELINGS...

MY DREAM AND WISH...

DATE: _____

WHAT I LEARNED TODAY...

WHAT I WANT TO LEARN TO DO AND TO BE BETTER AT...

MY CREATIVE IDEAS AND PROJECTS...

PLAN AND ACTION (What I need to do to make it happen)...

DATE: _____

I AM GRATEFUL FOR...

MY THOUGHTS AND FEELINGS...

MY DREAM AND WISH...

DATE: _____

WHAT I LEARNED TODAY...

WHAT I WANT TO LEARN TO DO AND TO BE BETTER AT...

MY CREATIVE IDEAS AND PROJECTS...

PLAN AND ACTION (What I need to do to make it happen)...

DATE: _____

I AM GRATEFUL FOR...

MY THOUGHTS AND FEELINGS...

MY DREAM AND WISH...

DATE: _____

WHAT I LEARNED TODAY...

WHAT I WANT TO LEARN TO DO AND TO BE BETTER AT...

MY CREATIVE IDEAS AND PROJECTS...

PLAN AND ACTION (What I need to do to make it happen)...

DATE: _____

I AM GRATEFUL FOR...

MY THOUGHTS AND FEELINGS...

MY DREAM AND WISH...

DATE: _____

WHAT I LEARNED TODAY...

WHAT I WANT TO LEARN TO DO AND TO BE BETTER AT...

MY CREATIVE IDEAS AND PROJECTS...

PLAN AND ACTION (What I need to do to make it happen)...

DATE: _____

I AM GRATEFUL FOR...

MY THOUGHTS AND FEELINGS...

MY DREAM AND WISH...

DATE: _____

WHAT I LEARNED TODAY...

WHAT I WANT TO LEARN TO DO AND TO BE BETTER AT...

MY CREATIVE IDEAS AND PROJECTS...

PLAN AND ACTION (What I need to do to make it happen)...

DATE: _____

I AM GRATEFUL FOR...

MY THOUGHTS AND FEELINGS...

MY DREAM AND WISH...

DATE: _____

WHAT I LEARNED TODAY...

WHAT I WANT TO LEARN TO DO AND TO BE BETTER AT...

MY CREATIVE IDEAS AND PROJECTS...

PLAN AND ACTION (What I need to do to make it happen)...

DATE: _____

I AM GRATEFUL FOR...

MY THOUGHTS AND FEELINGS...

MY DREAM AND WISH...

DATE: _____

WHAT I LEARNED TODAY...

WHAT I WANT TO LEARN TO DO AND TO BE BETTER AT...

MY CREATIVE IDEAS AND PROJECTS...

PLAN AND ACTION (What I need to do to make it happen)...

DATE: _____

I AM GRATEFUL FOR...

MY THOUGHTS AND FEELINGS...

MY DREAM AND WISH...

DATE: _____

WHAT I LEARNED TODAY...

WHAT I WANT TO LEARN TO DO AND TO BE BETTER AT...

MY CREATIVE IDEAS AND PROJECTS...

PLAN AND ACTION (What I need to do to make it happen)...

Made in the USA
Columbia, SC
17 April 2022